Stress
Can Really
Get on Your
Nerves

Trevor Romain & Elizabeth Verdick

Illustrated by Steve Mark

free spirit
PUBLISHING®

Library of Congress Cataloging-in-Publication Data
Names: Romain, Trevor, author. | Verdick, Elizabeth, author. | Mark, Steve, illustrator.
Title: Stress can really get on your nerves! / by Trevor Romain & Elizabeth Verdick ; illustrated by Steve Mark.
Description: Revised & updated edition. | Minneapolis, MN : Free Spirit Publishing Inc., [2018] | Series: Laugh & learn | Includes index. | Identifiers: LCCN 2017041581 (print) | LCCN 2017048710 (ebook) | ISBN 9781631982460 (Web PDF) | ISBN 9781631982477 (ePub) | ISBN 9781631982453 (pbk.) | ISBN 1631982451 (pbk.)
Subjects: LCSH: Stress in children—Juvenile literature. | Stress management for children—Juvenile literature. | Stress in adolescence—Juvenile literature. | Stress management for teenagers—Juvenile literature.
Classification: LCC BF723.S75 (ebook) | LCC BF723.S75 R66 2018 (print) | DDC 155.9/042—dc23
LC record available at https://lccn.loc.gov/2017041581

Reading Level 5; Interest Level Ages 8–13;
Fountas & Pinnell Guided Reading Level T

Cover and interior design by Shannon Pourciau
Edited by Eric Braun

10 9 8 7 6 5 4
Printed in China
R18861021

Free Spirit Publishing Inc.
6325 Sandburg Road, Suite 100
Minneapolis, MN 55427–3674
(612) 338-2068
help4kids@freespirit.com
freespirit.com

Dedication

This book is dedicated to our families who, with their loving support, helped us not stress out while putting it together.

Contents

Test Your Stress

Before you read the rest of the book, take this fun test. And don't worry! You automatically get an A just for answering the questions.

1. At night, do you have dreams about getting chased, taking a test where you don't know any answers, or standing in front of a bunch of people without your clothes on? Yes○ or No○

2. Does the thought of going to school ever worry you so much you could almost puke?
Yes○ or No○

3. Does your head sometimes feel like it's being squeezed by a boa constrictor?
Yes○ or No○

4. Does your to-do list seem a mile long?
Yes○ or No○

5. Would a good nickname for you be "Grouchy McStress"? Yes○ or No○

6. Do you ever wish for a magic wand to make your stress—POOF—disappear? Yes○ or No○

7. Some days, do you walk around so tired that you feel like you're on "autopilot"?
Yes○ or No○

8. Are you often so tense that your shoulders are up to your ears? Yes○ or No○

9. Do you wish aliens would capture you, so you could escape from your problems?
Yes○ or No○

10. Are you sometimes as jumpy as a rubber ball bouncing off the ceiling? Yes○ or No○

11. Does the world ever seem to be spinning so fast that you want to get off for a moment and take a break? Yes○ or No○

How Did You Do?

If you answered **yes** to all or most of these questions, you are *stressed out*. This book can help.

If you answered **yes** to some of the questions, you can use this book to deal with stressful days.

If you answered **no** to all of the questions, you're cool as a cucumber. Keep reading to learn how to stay that way.

Here's your **A** . . .

Chapter 1

What the Heck Is Stress?

Stress is what you feel when

1. situations make you uncomfortable

or

2. you're worried about something that has happened, will happen, or *might* happen.

That STRESS Feeling:

Seems to take over your mind and body, and causes . . .

Tension in your muscles. It's a . . .

Reaction to things that are new, scary, or different. It's . . .

Especially common in kids who are shy, have many pressures at home or school, or want to be "the best." It's also a . . .

Source of headaches and stomachaches. And it's . . .

Something lots of kids don't recognize until they understand the symptoms.

Stress can cause you to be so anxious that your body sends you weird and mixed-up signals. Believe it or not, you may find yourself sweating in a cold room or shivering on a hot day. You might even feel as if you're crawling out of your own skin.

Here are words to describe that STRESS feeling:

ALL ALONE uptight MOODY

CRABBY TIRED OUT

FREAKED OUT JITTERY QUEASY

ANXIOUS

nervous

goose-bumpy burned out

PANICKY EXCITED

JUMPY

CONFUSED

WIRED pressured

Different Types of Stress

Sometimes stress hits you all at once, like someone poured a bucket of water over your head. But sometimes stress is SNEAKY. It slowly creeps up, and you sense something's wrong but you don't know what it is.

Then there's the stress that just won't go away. It's been around so long that it's almost like a member of the family.

Stress takes its job verrrrrrry seriously. Look at all the things it's responsible for:

STRESS'S
JOB DESCRIPTION

- Keep kids up all night with worry.
- Make them wake up feeling tired and tense.
- Give them a sick feeling in their stomach and head.
- Cause them to feel sad, angry, helpless, alone, or upset.
- Make them anxious about life.
- Make it harder for them to do well in school, have fun, or try new activities.
- Get them to scream and yell, or take out their feelings on other people.
- Make them want to run and hide.
- Convince them there's no such word as *relax*.

A Few Facts About Stress

You can't wish stress away or pretend it's not there. Stress doesn't like to be ignored.

(No wonder it can *really* get on your nerves.)

Stress isn't your mom or dad. You don't have to do what it tells you to do.

Stress isn't a subject you *have* to take at school. And it's not a social media message you have to answer.

Best of all:

YOU are the boss of your stress—not the other way around.

Chapter 2
Why, Oh, Why, Do We Have Stress?

Stress can be measured in levels. How stressed are you right now?

A little stress isn't bad. Sometimes you might feel excited or energized by stress. For example, knowing your homework is due gives you that extra push you need to get it done. Feeling pumped up about your soccer match can help you play better. And realizing that your violin recital will take place soon might help you feel more eager to practice. (This is called "good stress" or "normal stress.")

THiNK aBout thesE "T-times."

Tests

Tryouts

Taking on a new challenge

At times like these, your stress can sharpen your mind and body . . . *Temporarily.*

In such situations, you might feel excited and focused or get the sensation of butterflies in your stomach. A boost like this can help you reach your goal. Think of it as "stress juice."

Then, when you're done with whatever was stressing you out, you feel like yourself again. (Maybe a little extra *Tired.*)

So, how do you tell the difference between good stress and bad stress? Read on.

Pinpoint Your Stress

Stress sets off alarms in your brain and body. The moment you sense something that puts you at risk: BEEP-BEEP-BEEP-BEEP! Hello, Stress.

Experts have a term for the response: FIGHT, FLIGHT, or FREEZE.

In other words, the stress causes your body to protect itself by fighting, fleeing, or freezing. Your reaction isn't something you plan out. You just do it.

This built-in reaction has helped humans survive since prehistoric times. Imagine yourself as a cave person. There you are, innocently sharpening your spear, when a hungry saber-toothed tiger jumps out from behind a bush. ROAR!

If you just stood there doing nothing, you'd be . . . DEAD MEAT.

Lucky for you, your body and brain automatically know what to do. In a flash, your "fight-flight-freeze" response kicks in:

- Your heart beats harder and faster, so you can run or defend yourself.

- The blood rushes to your large muscles (the ones that help you flee or fight).
- Your body makes chemicals like adrenaline, which boost your energy.
- You start to sweat as your body gets ready to run or fight.
- Your stomach shuts down, so your blood can flow where it's needed most.

All of this happens so you can FIGHT that hungry tiger, FLEE (run away from it), or FREEZE (and hope it doesn't notice you).

So you can live to tell the story.

In a way, it's cool that your body has an automatic response to protect you. It's almost like you've activated some superpowers that help you react to danger. The only thing is, most of us aren't being chased by saber-tooth tigers—or even zippy little Chihuahuas. Today's stresses aren't the same as they were ages ago, when our "normal" stress response came in very handy.

Flash forward to the present. You're up against a deadly, dangerous . . .

PRESENTATION!

You stand up in front of the class, and—quick as lightning—your FIGHT, FLIGHT, or FREEZE response turns on. Even if you didn't ask it to.

Some of the following reactions may take place:

- You momentarily become tongue-tied or go blank.
- You break into a sweat.
- Your hands and feet get colder as the blood flows away from them.
- Blood rushes to your face.
- Your mouth gets dry.
- Your heart starts to race.
- Your stomach feels upset or filled with butterflies.
- You want to run and hide.
- You become a statue of yourself.

These reactions—though typical—aren't exactly helpful in THIS situation!

Modern Stress

Times have changed, but people's reactions to danger or stress are as strong as ever. To prove it, try this: Right now, close your eyes and imagine you're walking down a dark street all alone . . . then you hear footsteps behind you. And someone . . . or some*thing* . . . breathing. Feel a little nervous? Just thinking about a tense situation can set off your alarms.

The good news is you can learn to manage your stress symptoms. You have some power over stress. When you feel that urge to **FIGHT**, FLEE, or FREEZE, you can coach yourself into a response that actually works for the situation. With practice, you'll get better at it. This is a skill you can use all your life. You'll find tips for learning this skill in Chapter 4: How to Cope (Not Be a Dope). And if your stress is *really* a problem, take a look at Chapter 5: Become a Panic Mechanic.

Chapter 3
Sources O' Stress (SOS)

Lots of things can cause stress in kids' lives. Here are a few stressors:

- family troubles, conflicts with siblings
- lacking food, money, or shelter
- being teased about one's race, ethnicity, background, disability, appearance, and so on
- homework, tests, grades, and projects
- school in general
- fitting in, social worries, fights with friends
- kids who bully
- cliques
- busy schedules after school and on weekends
- expectations for teams, performance groups, or clubs
- fears about violence at home, at school, or in the community
- scary news about politics and a changing world
- worries about the environment and the planet

Do you feel anxious about some of these things? If you do, you're not alone.

Daily stresses at home and school are a part of life. But it's time to ask yourself if you think your stress is the helpful kind or something bigger.

Does Your Schedule Stress You Out?

These days, many kids are overscheduled. This means that their extracurricular activities and to-do lists are way too full. Does your after-school time look something like this?

Most days, do you find that you only have time to grab a quick snack on your way to your next activity? Do you eat entire meals while being driven from one place to the next? Do you keep lots of extra clothes and gear handy because you don't have time to go home and change in between activities? These are signs that you may have too many commitments on your schedule. Let your mom or dad know if you're overloaded. Which activities can you cut back?

Do You Have Techno Stress?

Some kids find that technology is a stressor in their lives.

- Maybe you want a cell phone or tablet like your friends have but can't get one.
- Maybe it's stressful when you watch violent shows or movies.
- Perhaps the time you spend gaming adds up to stress, because you've played too long, you don't like how you did, or your adrenaline level got too high.
- Maybe social media is a stressor because you've been teased or bullied online.
- Or perhaps just keeping up with social media stresses you out.

These kinds of stressors are fairly new for people, so experts are still learning about technology's effects. One thing that's known: The effects on kids and teens can be serious. As in: kids who use a lot of technology have a harder time socializing face-to-face and trouble with paying attention—*and* higher stress levels.

So, it's probably no surprise that adults set guidelines for your screen-time each day. (Even if those same adults have a lot of screen-time themselves!)

Here's the Scoop:

Experts say that families should work together to plan a set of screen-time rules that work for the kids and adults in the family. When making a plan, consider ALL screens, including phones, tablets, TVs, movies, computers, and so on.

It might seem like chilling out with technology *relieves* stress. But it can have the opposite result. Keep a log—an honest one—that counts the number of minutes or hours you spend in front of screens each day. Is it more than you thought? Is it interfering with important things like homework, chores, or sleep? If you need to cut back, you can make a tech schedule for yourself, with help from your family.

Our Family Media Plan

SCREEN-*FREE* TIMES

When the family is together talking or playing games

During meals

One hour before bedtime

In the car, except during long trips

EXAMPLES OF POSITIVE SCREEN USE

Video chatting with relatives and friends

Watching educational TV shows or movies

Doing homework or visiting teachers' websites

INSTEAD OF USING SCREENS, WE CAN

Exercise

Talk

Read aloud together

Work on a family project

Play board games or do puzzles

Play outside

BONUS: Exercising and getting outside in the fresh air are great stress-busters!

Does the News Make You Nervous?

The news is everywhere. You see news on television or online. News stories may appear on your social media. You read and hear about news events when you're in school. Your family probably talks about events happening locally and around the world. And that news? It's not always good.

Many adults feel overwhelmed and upset by negative news. You soak up their stress—and of course feel your *own* stress, too. Even if a sad or scary news event doesn't affect you personally, you might still feel worry and pain. Because you CARE about what happens to other people, whether they live close to your home or far away. And part of you may think: What if something bad happens to my family or to me? Am I safe?

A sense of safety and peace is important. Talk to the adults in your life about news events that stress you out. Ask:

What do I do when things feel out of control?

What can we all do to make life better for ourselves and the people (and animals) in our community?

How do we stay hopeful and positive when we know others are hurting?

There are no easy answers. Talking helps—but taking action is even better. Can you reach out to others through volunteering your time? Or join a social-issues club at school? Can you make posters to spread awareness of causes you care about—or posters to share *good* news? How about making donations to organizations that do positive work? Cleaning up litter? Encouraging more recycling at home or school? When you do something, even something small, you feel more in control—and less stressed.

Staying hopeful is a stress-reliever, too! Make a point of finding good news—stories about people helping, stories about hope. Read books about heroes. Find

biographies of people who fought for a cause, marched in a peaceful protest, or did something else to change the world for the better. Write down quotes that make you feel brave or help you see the bright side of life. Find other kids who care about what *you* care about— work together to make a positive difference.

A Final Tip

Create a list of the stressors in your life. When you put your worries on paper, they get out of your head for a while. That feeling of "What if, what if, what if?" can start to settle down.

Chapter 4
How to Cope (Not Be a Dope)

Stress can make **ANYONE** worried, nervous, and upset. (Including grown-ups.) When you feel anxious, it's natural to want to run for the nearest exit. Plenty of kids have tried to do just that. Read on.

Strange-But-True Tales

Rosa* was nervous about playing volleyball in front of the other kids. She thought she'd miss the ball and everyone would yell at her. To get out of the game, she asked a friend to help her create a fake injury with makeup. When they were done, Rosa showed her newly black-and-blue finger (and not-too-real-looking bandage) to the gym teacher—who wasn't exactly fooled.

When Jarvis was at summer camp for the first time, he didn't want to admit he was anxious about being away from his family. He got so stressed out that he started to feel sick. In the nurse's office, he wrote long letters to his parents, begging to come home. He even tried to raise his temperature by lying under a bunch of blankets in the summer heat. But Jarvis didn't get sent home—and he spent most of camp in bed.

*These stressed-out kids are real—their names aren't.

Malik was getting bullied at school. The school had done presentations about bullying, and teachers wanted a bully-free classroom. But not all the kids listened or cared. Malik knew one of the worst places was the boys' bathroom, where kids had cornered him one too many times. His solution? Not to go to the bathroom all day *every* day. He'd hold it in and be so uncomfortable he could hardly wait to get home.

Lexy was one of the fastest runners in school. One day during gym, the class went outside for the 100-yard dash. She wanted to win more than anything. But right before the race, Lexy got nervous and felt too scared to compete. She pretended to hurt her ankle and then faked a limp. In the excitement of watching the races, she forgot what she was doing. Some of the other kids noticed and called out:

Escape Plans That Backfire

Maybe you've tried to get out of stressful situations by running away or faking that you're sick or hurt. For example, have you ever pretended to be ill on a day you had a test? (This is pretty common for kids to do.) Maybe you stayed on the couch watching TV instead of going to school. You escaped—what a relief!

Or *did* you? You eventually had to take that test. And while you were studying for it later, you may have fallen behind on your other work, causing even more tension. Avoiding the things you need to do doesn't actually help you avoid stress.

BAD Escape Plan #1: Skipping school. Not a good idea. Sooner or later, you get caught—and detention is no fun.

BAD Escape Plan #2: Using food to cope. Candy, doughnuts, chips, and fast food are more tempting during stressful times. But eating lots of sugary, salty treats puts more stress on your body. Same goes for sodas and other sugary drinks.

BAD Escape Plan #3: Getting lost in video games.
(Or phone apps, social media, or texting all night long.)
If you're too into your tech time, you're not working
on fixing the true sources of your stress. Find healthier
ways to address your stress.

BAD Escape Plan #4: Using drugs and alcohol.
Getting drunk or high doesn't solve problems—it
creates more.

What can you do instead of trying to escape? *Put your worries into words*. But *not* these kinds of words:

When you're tense and upset, you may feel like shouting at everyone. But shouting won't make your stress go away. Stress comes right back—like a boomerang. LOOK OUT!

Tell someone what's bothering you and ask for help. You might say:

"I'm really stressed out, and I don't know what to do. Can you help me?"

Talk to friends, parents, relatives, teachers, school counselors, a youth group leader, a religious advisor, your family doctor, or your principal. If talking to someone face-to-face isn't possible or comfortable, you could write a letter or an email. You could also text someone who's likely to respond.

The World's Worst Stress Relievers*

Banging your head against a wall won't help you feel less stressed. All this will do is give you a large lump and a bad headache.

Breaking things won't reduce your stress level either. If your stuff is broken, this will annoy you even more.

*Warning: Don't try these. Seriously!

Swearing won't get you anywhere but in trouble! Kicking bricks will only hurt your foot.

Blaming everything and everyone but yourself won't get you very far.

"you MADE me yell at you!"

"I didn't make the goal because my shoelace was untied."

"It's all my teacher's fault I got a bad grade."

Taking out your stress on an animal is hurtful—to both of you. Your pet doesn't understand the word *stress*. All a pet wants is love.

Stuffing your noisy little brother in the closet will **NOT** reduce your stress. (If you're busy and a brother or sister is bugging you, talk to a parent.)

NO!!! Cigarettes *don't* help you feel relaxed and refreshed! Smoking is more like standing in a smelly cloud of truck exhaust while licking an old rubber tire.

When you're stressed out, wound up, freaked out, or fed up, it's time to **CHILL OUT**. You have the power to put stress in its place. All you need are the right tools.

Chapter 5
Become a Panic Mechanic

A mechanic fixes your car. A Panic Mechanic fixes your stress. (This is very different from a Volcanic Mechanic—who only makes things worse!)

If you're stressed out, you can become your own Panic Mechanic—which means you look at what's wrong (your Stress Mess) and use your tools to make repairs.

Stress Mess #1: You're restless, frantic, and jumpy as a frog.

TOOL: Balance out your energy.

Stress produces lots of extra energy in your body. Do something positive with it! Run with your dog or go skateboarding, for example. If you're jittery at school, ask your teacher if you can take a bathroom break. Walk quickly (but quietly) down the hall and do some stretches in the restroom. Moving your body will help *balance out* the bad energy.

Stress Mess #2: You're so stressed out, everything annoys you. Even a little noise or movement makes you want to scream.

TOOL: Look for ways to find quiet.

Take some time alone to calm down. Go to your bedroom or the basement, or make a secret hideaway using a table and some blankets. Put on some headphones. You may even enjoy closing your eyes and imagining you're someplace peaceful: a tree house, a wooded path, or outside during a snowfall.

Stress Mess #3: Stressing out leads to spacing out.

Five minutes later:

TOOL: BREATHE DEEPLY.

If you catch yourself zoning out in class or during conversations, take a few deep breaths. This brings oxygen to your brain and helps you think better. If possible, go outside for fresh air.

Stress Mess #4: You worry almost all the time—even about things that aren't likely to happen.

TOOL: CLIMB ABOVE YOUR STRESS.

All that worrying shows that you've got a good imagination! Use it to do something creative like draw, write a story, make up a dance, design a website, or work on a comedy routine. Focusing on something fun helps push the worries out of your mind.

Stress Mess #5: You feel like stress is the boss of your life.

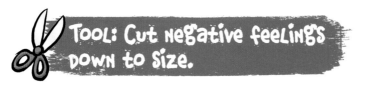

TOOL: Cut Negative Feelings Down to Size.

Stress can be overwhelming. You may feel like you can't handle things anymore. Don't push the panic button! **You** are bigger than your stress. Tell yourself that you're going to find ways to shrink your stress level.

See the stress-cutting ideas on the next page.

Quick Fixes for Stressful Days

- Spend time alone in a quiet place.
- Listen to soothing music or your favorite tunes.
- **Relax with your friends.**
- Go for a long walk or run around outside. Yoga can help, too.
- Play a musical instrument or do something else artistic.
- Enjoy a favorite hobby—or start a new one.
- Watch a movie—not a scary one!
- Read a book or some magazine articles. Or find some funny jokes.
- **Practice deep breathing. Breathe in and imagine your breath is a wave: It comes in through your toes and washes up your body all the way to your head. As you breathe out, imagine the wave washing back down through your body, down to your toes, and out to sea. Do this a few times until you feel more peaceful.**

- Volunteer your time. Helping someone else is a great way to help yourself.

- Do some chores. (It may sound crazy, but jobs like raking leaves or cleaning your room can actually help you calm down. The routine nature of a chore is soothing. And you get something done!)

- Make a worry jar. If you're a worrywart and your fears bother you all day long, set aside a special time to write your worries on little slips of paper. When you see your worries written out, their power begins to fade. Trap them in a jar where they can't bother you as much.

- Love your pet. It's a proven fact that animals can lower people's stress levels. Play with your dog, pet your cat, listen to your bird chirp, or watch your fish swim. These are great ways to relax. If you don't have any pets, ask if you can spend time with a friend's dog, cat, or other pet.

Stress Mess #6: Stress makes you feel like your life is one **BIG** problem.

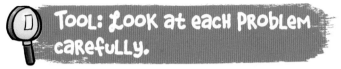

TOOL: Look at each Problem carefully.

When you're stressed, you have a general feeling that things aren't right in your life. You may lose sight of what was bothering you in the first place. Take some time to see the problem more clearly. Are you upset or worried about something in your life that's changed—or is about to change? Once you've spotted the problem, you can work on it.

Stress Mess #7: Worry makes you hurry.

TOOL: Slow Down.

Moving super fast makes you **more** anxious. And doing 16 things at once can stress you out too much. (For example, don't try to do homework while also eating dinner, texting, watching TV, and feeding your gerbil.) It's okay to do one thing at a time—and take your time doing it. Life doesn't have to be a race.

Stress Mess #8: You're so stressed about everything you have to do that you can't do *any* of it.

TOOL: Make a to-do list.

Lots of people get stressed out because they're overwhelmed with all that they have to accomplish. Making a to-do list or using a daily planner can help you feel less panicky. Start by listing all your tasks. Now rank them in order of importance. Does the first job on your list seem impossible? Break it down into chunks. Ready to tackle it? If not, break it down some more. *Now* does it seem possible? If it does, then complete the first task on your list. After that, take a short break to reward yourself. Now you're ready for the next task.

Stress Mess #9: You're so stressed out that you feel all twisted up—tight and tense from head to toe.

TOOL: Loosen the tension.

Stress leads to excess muscle tension, making you feel achy, stiff, or stretched to your limit. If you feel this way, try a relaxation exercise to loosen the tension. You'll find one starting on the next page.

Relax in 10 Easy Steps

This relaxation exercise is easy to learn. Read through the steps before you give it a try.

1. Find a quiet place where you won't be disturbed. (If possible, go outdoors—to the yard or to the park, for example. The fresh air will feel good.)

2. Lie down on the grass (or on the floor). Get comfortable.

3. Close your eyes, but don't fall asleep.

4. Breathe deeply. Focus on your breath going in and out. Count to five as you breathe in; count backward from five as you breathe out. Take your time.

5. When you feel calmer, continue the deep breathing, but as you breathe out, say the word *relax* in your mind.

6. In time with your breathing, begin to relax your muscles from head to toe. Start with your forehead. Tense those muscles as you breathe in, then relax them as you breathe out.

7. Continue tensing and relaxing—moving downward to your shoulders, arms, hands, stomach, legs, and feet. Each time, breathe in as you tense the muscles, and breathe out as you relax them.

8. Once you've reached your toes, take a rest. Keep breathing deeply.

9. Slowly open your eyes. Think: *I am now relaxed.*

10. Enjoy this feeling!

You can do the exercise any time you want to feel calmer. Remember the FIGHT, FLIGHT, or **FREEZE** response (see pages 25–29)? It has an opposite: REST and DIGEST. This means your muscles are relaxed, your mind is clear, and your stomach is open for business again. Relaxation helps you get there!

Stress Mess #10: You're so frantic you lose track of what's really important.

TOOL: Get Some Perspective.

Do you ever say things like, "If I don't make the team, I'll die!" or "I can't live without that pair of jeans!" Will these things actually kill you? Of course not! Telling yourself, "I might feel disappointed if I don't get what I want" is more realistic—and less stressful. Trying to see the big picture is a great way to lighten a stressful load.

Stress Mess #11: You feel like a big loser all the time.

TOOL: BRIGHTEN YOUR OUTLOOK.

What could be more stressful than constantly telling yourself how awful you are? If a little voice in your head is always putting you down, tell that voice to take a hike. Instead of, "Everyone will think I'm a loser," you can tell yourself, "I'm working hard and improving."

Here are a few other ways to turn negative thoughts into more positive ones.

Instead of saying . . .	Try saying . . .
I'll just make a mess of it.	Everyone makes mistakes.
I stink at science.	Science is not my best subject, but I'm good at others.
Everyone is better than me at soccer.	I'm trying hard and having fun—that's what's important.
I wish I had more friends.	I have people who love me and like to hang out with me.
I'll just embarrass myself.	I'm going to go for it!

Stress Mess #12: It seems like your life is spinning totally out of control.

TOOL: Use your safety net.

It's not just tightrope walkers who need safety nets. At some point, *everybody* needs someone to catch them when they're falling. Who do you trust with your problems? Who's a good listener and advice-giver? Find those people and ask for some help.

Chapter 6

Ways to Keep Stress at Bay Each Day

Now you know a lot about stress. You've figured out your own stressors and learned how to get help. But stress-busting isn't just a one-time thing. It's an **everyday** thing. Stress will pop up when you predict it—*and* when you least expect it. Even if you're on a sweet vacation.

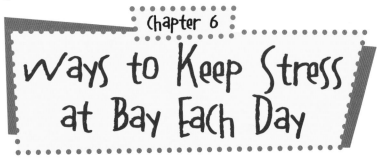

Stress is part of life: yours, ours, everyone's. Is that terrible news? Not necessarily. You have the power to make yourself strong enough to withstand day-to-day stress.

Give these daily tips a try . . . and kiss stress goodbye!

1. **Be active.** Exercise does more than help your body be healthy—it also lifts your spirits and helps you feel more relaxed. When you're active, you become stronger in your body and your mind. And that means you've got more power over stress.

2. **Eat right.** Eating food that's good for your body helps you stay healthy—and a healthy body is a better stress-fighter. Eat plenty of fruits, vegetables, whole grains, and protein. You can learn more about healthy eating at choosemyplate.gov. Or talk to your doctor or school nurse about your nutritional needs.

3. **Avoid caffeine.** This chemical—found mainly in drinks like soda, coffee, and tea—can make you feel edgy and tense. (It's like drinking pure stress—blech!)

4. **Get enough sleep.** It's hard to deal with stress if you're feeling tired and run down. During a good night's sleep, your mind and body recharge. This means you're sharper and stronger when you wake up. If you have trouble sleeping at night, talk to a parent or other adult you trust about the problem. You may need to get help from your doctor. Or maybe you just need to take a brief nap after school. But not *too* long of a nap because you want to get to sleep at bedtime.

5. **S-t-r-e-t-c-h.** When you wake up in the morning, *stretch*. Reach your arms to the sky and give your legs a chance to extend and warm up. Stretching *feels* good. It also helps revive your muscles or relax them when you're stressed. Yoga is a fun and relaxing daily practice for people of all ages. Join a class or learn about yoga and proper stretching from a DVD or online.

6. **Express your feelings.** Are you angry, sad, frustrated, jealous, hurt, or upset? Talk to someone or write about it. Locking up your feelings can add to your stress. You can also express emotions through physical activity and the arts.

7. **Be neat.** Do you have trouble remembering where you put your stuff? Kids' rooms are famous for swallowing things like toys, homework, charging cords, and secret notes—even the occasional peanut butter sandwich. Losing stuff can stress you out. Keeping your room clean and organized helps a lot. Same goes for your backpack or sports bag.

8. **Laugh it up.** Experts say laughter reduces stress. So memorize some jokes, read funny books, or see a live comedy show for kids. Giggling is good for you!

9. **Be a planner.** Feeling overwhelmed or like you're behind in everything? Time for some planning. Get a calendar and write down your projects, test dates, and other important stuff (or use a calendar app). Now make a homework and study schedule you can follow. A little advance planning will help you feel more in control of your days.

10. **Stand tall and firm.** Believe it or not, your posture can make a difference when it comes to stress. Are you slumped over? Leaning? Half asleep? Use your core muscles (your abdominals) to lift and hold yourself up. Straighten your spine, whether you're standing or sitting. Plant your feet firmly on the ground. *Feel* your strength. Now, smile and take a deep breath. These body cues are like a "power stance." They're an "I can do it" message to the world and yourself.

11. **Talk about your problems.** Who's a caring and trusted listener—your mom, your dad, a grandparent, your teacher, your best friend? Talk to that person. Share your problems. You'll feel better if you do.

12. **Forgive your mistakes.** Are you really hard on yourself every time you make a mistake? Beating yourself up over errors never helps. Instead, tell yourself that mistakes are learning experiences. (At least you know what *not* to do next time.) And guess what? Lots of people look back and realize their mistakes helped them build courage and "grit." You grow stronger from all your experiences—the good ones and the bad.

13. Be yourself. Trying to be something you're not just to keep up with the "cool" people can cause a lot of stress. Is there a better way? Sure! Simply being *you*—and being happy with your own brand of cool.

14. Feel good about what you have. Wanting expensive clothes and gadgets your family can't afford may leave you feeling like you never have enough. Instead of thinking about everything you want, take a moment to think about everything you *already have*. Make a list of what you're grateful for. You may quickly see that some of the best things in life don't cost money: a loving family, people who care about you, a dog licking your face, a sunny day. Keeping a daily "gratitude list" is a stress-buster.

Stress can really get on your nerves—but now you know what to do when it does. You can understand where stress comes from. You can be a Panic Mechanic and relieve much of the stress in your life. And no matter what's happening or how you feel, you can always take a deep breath and calm down. Stick to your stress-reducing plans, so stress won't get the best of you!

A Note for Parents and Teachers

In today's fast-paced, pressured world, more kids than ever are stressed out. But many kids don't understand what stress is (though they *feel* it), and many adults don't realize that kids can experience stress at a high level. Parents may think being stressed is a condition reserved for adults with grown-up responsibilities and obligations. Some parents may not realize that the responsibilities and obligations of being a kid can weigh just as heavily and cause just as much anxiety.

Stress in kids can stay hidden because the symptoms in children are usually *physical*. They may have symptoms of stress—headaches, stomachaches, trouble sleeping, lack of appetite—but because they don't know what stress is, they may think they're just getting sick. And because many adults assume that kids don't truly experience stress, they may treat these symptoms as signs of physical illness—which doesn't "cure" the symptoms because it doesn't address the cause.

Some kids experiencing stress wonder if something is wrong with them—but they don't want to talk about it because they think no one will understand. And some kids who are coping with chronic stress have symptoms that embarrass them.

Examples:

- wanting to cry all the time
- being frightened of the world
- feeling scared of the dark or of strangers
- worrying that something terrible will happen
- wetting the bed
- not wanting to be alone
- having nightmares
- feeling helpless

What can *you* do to help kids deal with stress? Start by recognizing that stress is very real for kids—it can be a big part of their lives. Look for signs of hidden or "secret" stress. Are there physical symptoms? Is their school performance suffering? What about their relationships with friends and family? When stress starts affecting kids' everyday lives, this gives them even *more* to worry about and makes them feel *more* stressed. Caring, aware adults can break this cycle.

Here are specific things you can do to help kids with their stress:

- Provide them with a safe, familiar, consistent environment.

- Make sure they have a dependable routine.

- Encourage them to talk openly about their feelings and problems.

- Listen if they confide their worries or fears.

- Offer affection and understanding, never criticism, if they express anxiety.

- Become more aware of the causes of their stress (new experiences, fear of failure, change, loss).

- Create a screen-time schedule so you're on top of the role technology plays in their lives.

- Talk about upcoming changes and challenges at home and school.

- If appropriate, discuss difficult events occurring in your community or worldwide that may affect kids. Often, they're aware of what's in the news but they aren't sure if they should ask questions. Show that you're open and willing to address their concerns.

- Spend time being calm and relaxed together outdoors whenever possible.

- Make sure they're physically active and eat healthy foods.

- Encourage them to get enough sleep.

- Help them prepare the night before, so mornings aren't too rushed.

- Give them a chance to make choices, so they have some control over their lives.

- Help them build their self-esteem by encouraging them to be proud of who they are.

- Recognize kids' strengths and help them build on these qualities.

- Involve them in situations or activities where they have a good chance of succeeding.

- Ask yourself if your expectations of them are too high, leading to increased pressure in their lives. Is your child overscheduled? Kids need downtime to play, relax, and explore the outdoor world.

- Give them a chance to help others because helping others creates feelings of warmth and value. Volunteer together in your community or through the school, and donate to causes your child supports.

- Seek professional help, if needed, by consulting a doctor, psychologist, counselor, or social worker.

Even young children can learn to recognize the signs of stress and begin resolving situations that are causing problems for them. Reading this book is a good first step. You might want to read it with your child or your class and allow time for questions and discussion.

Index

About the Authors and Illustrator

Trevor Romain is an award-winning author and illustrator as well as a sought-after motivational speaker. His books have sold more than a million copies and have been published in 18 languages. For more than 20 years, Trevor has traveled throughout the world, speaking to thousands of school-age children. Trevor is well known for his work with the Make-A-Wish Foundation, the United Nations, UNICEF, USO, and the Comfort Crew for Military Kids, which he co-founded. Trevor lives in Austin, Texas.

Elizabeth Verdick helped create the Free Spirit Publishing Laugh & Learn series and is the author of many books for children and teens. She lives in Minnesota with her husband, two children, and a houseful of pets.

Steve Mark is a freelance illustrator and a part-time puppeteer. He lives in Minnesota and is the father of three and the husband of one. Steve has illustrated all the books in the Laugh & Learn series, including *Don't Behave Like You Live in a Cave* and *Bullying Is a Pain in the Brain*.